SALES & MARKETING MASTERY

Winning Strategies for Business Growth

Kate Bush

Table of Contents

Introduction

Importance Of Sales And Marketing Strategies.

Any profitable firm must have strong sales and monthly plans. Here is a quick summary of their significance:

1. Revenue Generation: Revenue generation is essentially the responsibility of sales and marketing. Effective methods immediately affect the bottom line by bringing in clients, generating leads, and turning prospects into paying customers.

2. Customer Acquisition: Sales methods clinch transactions, while marketing strategies assist in finding and targeting prospective customers. Together, they guarantee a constant flow of new customers.

3. Market Expansion: Sales and marketing tactics help businesses develop and expand by accessing new audiences and markets, allowing them to take advantage of unexplored possibilities.

4. Brand Awareness: Familiarity and trust are developed via marketing, which makes it simpler for sales teams to convert leads. Premium rates may likewise be demanded by a powerful brand.

5. Competitive Advantage: Well-designed tactics may set a company apart from rivals, whether via cutting-edge marketing campaigns or distinctive sales techniques.

6. Customer Retention: Marketing involves more than simply attracting clients; it also involves keeping them. The need for ongoing customer acquisition efforts is diminished by effective marketing that fosters customer loyalty.

7. Data-Driven Decision-Making: To hone their tactics, sales and marketing both depend on data. Future choices are influenced by analysis of consumer behavior, sales trends, and marketing ROI.

8. Cost-Effectiveness: Simplified marketing and sales tactics make ensuring that resources are used effectively, cutting down on the wastage of both time and money.

9. Shifting to Market Changes: Sales and marketing strategies must be adaptable and sensitive to shifting consumer preferences and competitive environments in a market that is evolving rapidly.

10. Long-Term Goals: A well-executed sales and marketing strategy lays the groundwork for long-term corporate success by guaranteeing sustainability and profitability.

In essence, a company's sales and marketing tactics are what keep it growing, profitable, and customer-focused. Any firm hoping to succeed in a cutthroat market has to have these methods working in harmony.

Chapter 1

Target Audience Research

In the world of sales and marketing, having an understanding of your audience is equivalent to having the key to success. It involves penetrating the minds and hearts of the people you want to influence.

This grasp goes well beyond a cursory look at demographics to include a thorough appreciation of people's wants, needs, and goals.

With this information at your disposal, your message changes from impersonal noise into a customized symphony of answers. You may cater to their particular requirements, create gripping storylines, and provide exactly what they're looking for.

Additionally, knowing your target helps you allocate resources effectively, ensuring that your marketing initiatives are successful without squandering time and money. It creates the foundation for genuine interactions that make clients feel seen and heard and promote satisfaction and loyalty.

This knowledge gives you an advantage in a competitive market. You can innovate, communicate clearly, and establish trust thanks to it. It shapes your plans and ensures long-term success by enabling data-driven choices.

In essence, knowing your audience is the compass that steers you through the murky seas of sales and marketing and leads you to a successful destination.

It's not only about getting in front of people; it's also about making deep connections that result in lasting bonds and mutual gain.

Researching The Market

The compass that directs firms on their path to success is market research. This is why it's an essential action:

1. Making Well-Informed Decisions: Market research offers data-driven insights that assist companies in making well-informed choices on product development, pricing, and marketing tactics.

2. Finding Possibilities: Market inefficiencies and unmet consumer demands are revealed through research, which creates room for creativity and new market possibilities for goods and services.

3. Targeted Marketing: By clearly defining their target market, organizations can develop marketing strategies that connect with consumers and increase engagement and conversion rates.

4. Risk Mitigation: Research assists in identifying prospective issues and market hazards, enabling companies to create plans to reduce them.

5. Competitive Advantage: Businesses may stand out from the competition and acquire a competitive advantage by having a thorough grasp of the market and their customers.

6. Optimizing Resources: Market research directs resource allocation to where it will have the most impact, preventing resources from being squandered on unsuccessful methods.

7. Long-Term Success: Continuous research guarantees that companies remain aware of market changes and client preferences, ensuring their long-term success.

8. Customer Retention: Understanding the aspects that influence customer happiness and loyalty may assist in maintaining current clients, who often turn into brand evangelists.

9. Data-Driven Growth: Growth plans are informed by data from market research, allowing organizations to diversify into new markets or enhance their current ones.

In conclusion, market research serves as the cornerstone for the development of successful companies. It's a continuing commitment to keep in touch with clients, rival businesses, and the always-shifting market environment. In a fast-paced corporate climate, it's essential to reach sustainable development, reduce risks, and make educated choices.

Persona Creation: Knowing Your Audience

The process of developing buyer personas is comparable to constructing the characters in a novel in the worlds of marketing and product development.

These fictitious personas serve as a representation of your ideal clients and are essential to the development of your tactics.

The following describes why persona creation is crucial:

1. Humanizing Data: Personas humanize data by turning it into relatable humans with names, faces, and biographies. Data becomes more understandable and usable via humanization.

2. Focused Targeting: Personas provide you the ability to target your marketing campaigns with extreme precision. You are aware of the person you are speaking with, their interests, and where to locate them.

3. Relevant Message: Personas make your message more relevant and compelling. You speak directly to the needs, wants, and goals of your ideal clients.

4. Product Alignment: Personas direct the creation of products and services. You ensure product-market fit by developing offers that specifically meet the demands of your personas.

5. Problem-Solving: Personas are your compass when it comes to problem-solving. You have a thorough understanding of their problems and can make solutions specific to them.

6. Creation of Content: When content is produced with personalities in mind, it becomes meaningful. You create material for your target audience that informs, amuses, or addresses issues.

7. Channel Selection: Personas guide your decision on the marketing channels you use. You are aware of the online activities your personas engage in, whether they be on social media, email, or business forums.

8. Building Empathy: Creating personas encourages empathy inside your business. Teams acquire a better understanding of the clients they support.

9. Consensus Building: Personas help cross-functional teams reach agreement by facilitating consensus-building. Everyone is aware of their employer and the purpose of their labor.

10. Continuous Improvement: Personas change as your company and the market do. They enable you to remain flexible and responsive to changing client demands.

Persona building is really about giving your data a face and developing empathy for your audience. It's a tool that enables you to develop customized, effective plans that connect with actual people and convert prospects into devoted consumers.

Adapting Marketing Activities: Reaching Your Audience

Effective marketing requires developing methods that connect with your target audience rather than taking a one-size-fits-all approach. You should personalize your marketing efforts for the following reasons:

1. Relevance: Tailored marketing directly addresses the wants and preferences of your target market. It's about demonstrating your understanding of them, which increases engagement.

2. Personalization: Based on data and insights, personalized marketing increases the chance of conversion by giving consumers a sense of worth and appreciation.

3. Engagement: Engagement rates are increased by customized content and messages since they seem more like a conversation than a broadcast.

4. Conversion: Marketing initiatives that are relevant to potential clients are more likely to result in sales and company expansion.

5. Customer Loyalty: Customers are more likely to stick with your brand and recommend it to others if they feel heard and taken care of.

6. Efficiency: By focusing your efforts on the right consumers, you may maximize your marketing budget and cut down on unnecessary expenditures.

7. Market Differentiation: Customized tactics set you distinct from rivals who could be using a one-size-fits-all strategy in the market.

8. Utilizing Data: Customized marketing makes choices based on data and insights, enhancing the effectiveness of your data-driven tactics.

9. Scalability: As your comprehension of your audience grows, you may expand the scope of your targeted marketing initiatives while maintaining customization.

10. Adaptability: Both audience tastes and market circumstances are always changing. With tailored marketing, you can respond quickly to these changes and maintain your relevance and competitiveness.

In conclusion, customizing marketing initiatives is the link that connects your brand with your audience. Speaking their language, addressing their issues, and forging a strong bond are all important.

Your marketing efforts will be more effective and meaningful if you consider how you provide your products and services in addition to what you do.

Chapter 2

Marketing Content

The Strength of Content

Imagine if your written and visual content had the power to persuade, interest, and inspire. Content serves that purpose perfectly.

It goes beyond just words and pictures; it serves as a means of expression, a storyteller, and a link between your business and your target market.

Think about how informational material translates difficult ideas into comprehensible concepts to teach and inform. It serves as a teacher, leading the audience on a quest for knowledge.

Consider how some types of material might inspire feelings like inspiration, empathy, or pleasure. It is a conductor of emotions, leaving its participants with lasting impressions on their hearts and thoughts.

When done well, content builds authority. It establishes your brand as an authority in your industry or particular area.

Content is the secret to exposure in the digital world. It is what drives prospective buyers to your door and makes your website discoverable.

But content involves more than just the mind; it also involves the emotions. Consistency and value help to create trust, resulting in the growth of enduring partnerships.

It serves as your persuasive buddy, assisting prospects on their transition from idly watching to devoted patrons.

In a sea of rival brands, content serves as your brand's voice and identity. It's your narrative, which establishes a personal connection between you and your audience.

The secret is that content persists. Long after it was created, it continues to captivate an audience and produce results, giving off enduring worth.

It's not simply the stuff you make in this digital age; it's also how you create it. Engaging content is more than simply informative material. It's emotional as well as utilitarian.

You'll use the impact, engagement, and connection-building capabilities of content as future sales and marketing professionals. You may use it to increase conversions, foster brand loyalty, and cultivate trust.

Keep in mind that in the always-changing world of sales and marketing, your words and images have the power to influence perceptions, evoke emotions, and promote success.

Content Types: Building Your Marketing Armory

Content takes in many different forms in the dynamic world of marketing, each with its function and ways to engage different facets of your audience.

Let's look at the many content categories that make up your marketing toolbox:

1. Blog Posts: Blog postings are a cornerstone of content marketing since they are enlightening and instructive. They provide in-depth insights, deal with problems, and build your authority in your area of expertise.

2. Social Media Posts: Social media material that is brief and to the point is ideal for interacting with your audience, offering updates, and starting discussions. Text, pictures, videos, and infographics are all included.

3. Videos: Video material is a potent tool for engagement and narrative. Explainer films, product demonstrations, interviews, or behind-the-scenes looks may all be used.

4. Infographics: These are visual representations of complicated information that are packed with facts and easy to understand. They work very well for communicating statistics and comparisons.

5. Ebooks and Guides: They are comprehensive resources that provide in-depth information on a variety of subjects. To gather email addresses, they often act as lead magnets.

6. Podcasts: Audio material is becoming more popular. Long-form conversations, interviews, and professional insights may all be heard on podcasts.

7. Case Studies: Use thorough case studies to highlight your successes. They show how your product or service may be used in actual situations.

8. Whitepapers: Detailed studies that examine market trends, scientific discoveries, or technical facets of your sector. Whitepapers establish your company's authority.

9. Email Marketing: Email campaigns provide tailored information right to the inboxes of your subscribers, increasing interaction and conversion rates.

10. Webinars: Interactive and instructive, webinars let you interact in real-time with your audience, disseminate information, and respond to inquiries.

11. User-Generated Content: Encourage your audience to provide material about your business, such as user-generated videos, reviews, or testimonials.

12. Interactive Content: Quizzes, surveys, and other interactive content engage your audience and gather insightful data.

13. Visual Content: Memes, GIFs, and visual narratives are useful for distributing humorous or relevant information on social media.

14. Live Streaming: Sites like Facebook Live and Instagram Live let you connect with viewers at the moment, giving your content a feeling of immediacy and authenticity.

15. Guest Posts: Promote industry influencers' or experts' material on your platforms or contribute to theirs to work together.

16. Press Releases: Use press releases to inform the public and the media about significant developments at your firm.

17. Product Descriptions: Product descriptions are crucial for e-commerce and sales sites because they must be thorough and compelling.

18. Testimonials and Reviews: To establish credibility and trust, highlight the good experiences of happy consumers.

19. Visual Stories: You may post transient material on websites like Instagram Stories and Snapchat, which gives it a genuine feel.

20. Interactive PDFs: A dynamic reading experience is provided by interactive PDFs, which are interesting documents that blend text, photos, and interactive features.

Your objectives, target audience, and the message you want to deliver will all influence the sort of material you choose.

Your marketing plan will be more successful if it uses a range of content formats to engage, educate, and convert your audience across channels and platforms.

Content Creation Techniques

Delivering value and engaging your audience are more important goals of content creation than just placing words on a page or photos on a screen.

Consider these efficient content-generation techniques:

1. Audience Research: Beginning with an awareness of the requirements, preferences, and pain points of your target audience, do audience research. The groundwork for information that resonates is laid forth in this study.

2. Content Calendar: Utilize a calendar to schedule your material in advance. It provides consistency and makes it easier to match your content to important events or seasonal patterns.

3. Keyword Research: To find relevant search phrases, use keyword research tools. To increase SEO and discoverability, organically include these keywords in your writing.

4. Storytelling: Create engrossing tales that hold your audience's attention. Stories arouse emotions, which enhances the retention and relatability of your material.

5. Quality Above Quantity: Prioritize producing high-quality material over producing a lot of it. Trust and loyalty are earned via valuable content.

6. Visual Appeal: Include eye-catching visuals like photos, infographics, and movies to increase visual appeal. Visual media is more appealing and easily shared.

7. Educational Content: By producing instructive material, you may spread your knowledge. You may establish yourself as an expert in your profession by writing how-to manuals, tutorials, and educational articles.

8. Variety: Diversify your content kinds, from blog posts and videos to podcasts and infographics, to accommodate a range of learning tastes and styles.

9. Consistency: Keep your tone, fashion, and publishing schedule constant. Consistency keeps your audience interested while also increasing brand identification.

10. Engagement: Encourage audience participation by posing queries, running polls, and swiftly answering messages and comments.

11. Relevance: The interests and current trends of your audience should be reflected in your material. To keep people interested, remain relevant.

Developing effective content requires flexibility, originality, and an awareness of your audience. By using these techniques, you can create content that engages and inspires your audience as well as educates them, eventually resulting in successful marketing.

Building Authority and Trust: The Foundations of Successful Marketing

Trust and authority are the cornerstones on which successful customer relationships and brand positioning are formed in the worlds of sales and marketing.

Here is how to create and maintain these fundamental components:

1.   Consistent   Quality: Deliver high-quality goods, services, and materials regularly to demonstrate your competency and dependability.

2. Transparency: Be upfront and truthful in all aspects of your company dealings, from price to communications. Trust is created through openness.

3. Prioritize Customers: Prioritize the demands and pleasures of your consumers by using a customer-centric approach. Happy consumers promote a brand.

4.   Expertise   Sharing: Share your industry knowledge with educational resources, webinars, and seminars to establish yourself as an authority.

5. Case Studies and Testimonials: To illustrate your track record, highlight actual success stories and reviews from happy clients.

6. Consistent Branding: Maintain a consistent brand identity and message across all channels to increase awareness and authority.

7. Ethical Practice: Maintain ethical standards in all facets of your firm to strengthen your dedication to dependability.

8. Community Engagement: Engage with your community, whether it is through taking on social responsibility projects or actively taking part in business events. It shows your commitment beyond financial gain.

You may develop authority and trust by using these tactics, which will help you build

a solid reputation and a following of devoted
clients.

Chapter 3

Email Marketing

Sending customized emails to a list of subscribers is a key component of the effective digital marketing tactic known as email marketing. It's a successful technique to develop customer connections, market goods and services, nurture leads, and encourage sales. Its effectiveness depends on personalization and segmentation, which make sure that receivers understand the communications.

Growing Your Email List

An effective marketing tool that gives you a direct channel of connection with your audience is an email list.

Here are some tips for expanding and building your email list:

1. Create Compelling Content: Provide readers with worthwhile stuff in return for their email addresses, such as ebooks, how-to manuals, or insider knowledge. Make sure the interests and requirements of your audience are reflected in your material.

2. Opt-In Forms: Placing opt-in forms on your website, landing pages, and blog posts should be done intelligently. Make it simple for visitors to subscribe by using brief, intuitive forms.

3. Landing Pages: Create specialized landing pages for certain offers or campaigns. These pages may only be used to collect email sign-ups.

4. Exit-Intent Pop-Ups: This shows up just when a visitor is ready to depart your website. Provide a strong incentive for subscribing, such as a discount or access to premium material.

5. Social Media Promotion: Promote your email sign-up on your social media channels by using the hashtag #socialmediapromotion. To encourage your audience to subscribe, emphasize the advantages.

6. Referral Programs: Encourage your existing subscribers to recommend friends and colleagues by offering referral programs. Provide awards or discounts as incentives for successful referrals.

7. Host Webinars or Virtual Events: Organizing webinars or online events might be a good approach to get email addresses. need participation through registration.

8. Contests and Giveaways: Run competitions or giveaways with an email sign-up as a criterion for admission. Make sure the award has some connection to your intended audience.

9. Segmentation: Segment your email list according to the demographics, interests, or actions of the subscribers. For more engagement, adapt your material to each section.

10. Personalization: Sending subscribers specific, targeted material and addressing them by name can personalize your email marketing.

11. Email Signature: Incorporate a CTA or link for email sign-up in your email signature. It's an often disregarded chance to bring in new subscribers.

14. Customer Surveys: Collect email addresses and obtain feedback by using questionnaires. Make sure you respect people's privacy and make your intentions clear.

16. Use Paid Advertising: Use sponsored advertising to encourage sign-ups by investing in paid advertising campaigns on Facebook or Google Ads.

Although it takes time and work to build an email list, it is a worthwhile investment for maintaining engagement with your audience, promoting conversions, and growing your business.

To keep your subscribers interested and happy, put your attention on offering value, protecting privacy, and regularly delivering relevant information.

Creating Successful Email Campaigns

Carefully prepared messages that are intended to engage and convert your audience make up effective email marketing.

How to make them is as follows:

1. Set Goals: Establish clear goals for your email campaign, whether they are to increase sales, nurture leads, or provide useful material.

2. Audience Segmentation: Divide your email list into parts depending on your audience's demographics, actions, or preferences. Make your communications specific to each group.

3. Catchy Headlines: Catch readers' attention with succinct, intriguing subject lines that motivate them to open your emails.

4. Personalization: Address recipients by name and personalize material depending on their preferences, previous interactions, or purchasing behavior.

5. Clear Call-To-Action (CTA): Specify the desired action you want recipients to do, whether it's making a purchase, signing up, or downloading material. This is known as a call-to-action (CTA).

6. Responsive Design: Make sure emails are mobile-friendly and have a layout that adjusts to various devices and screen sizes.

7. Engaging Information: Produce relevant, worthwhile information that appeals to your readers. Make use of pictures, narrative, and succinct writing.

8. A/B Testing: Test various aspects, including subject lines, CTAs, and images, to see which appeals to your audience the most.

9. Timing and Frequency: Send emails at the most effective intervals depending on the actions of your audience. Don't bombard them with too many emails.

10. Tracking and Analytics: Utilize monitoring software to monitor open rates, click-through rates, and conversions. Analyze the information to improve your next campaigns.

To provide communications that fascinate and convert subscribers, effective email campaigns strike a balance between creativity, personalization, and data-driven insights.

Maintaining Client Relationships

Any successful company depends on establishing and maintaining strong customer connections. It requires constant commitment rather than a one-time effort.

Here's an efficient way to go about it:

1. **Personalization:** Take into account user preferences while designing interactions and offerings.

2. Consistent Communication: Engagement will keep you interested with frequent updates and insightful material.

3. Responding Support: Offer quick help and issues.

4. Loyalty Programs: Loyal Consumers should be rewarded with incentives and exclusive deals via loyalty programs.

5. Feedback Loops: Utilize client input to improve your goods and services.

6. Transparency: Building trust via transparency in corporate processes.

7. Long-Term Focus: Give enduring connections a higher priority than instant gratification.

Building trust, providing great experiences, and showcasing your brand's sincere concern for its consumers are all important components of nurturing customer relationships.

This investment has the potential to generate repeat business, brand loyalty, and long-term success.

Chapter 4

Utilizing Social Media

Selecting the Appropriate Social Media Platforms

To interact and successfully reach your target audience, you must choose the appropriate social media channels for your company.

How to choose wisely is provided here:

1. Know Your Audience: Recognize the social media channels that your target audience likes to use. Platforms tend to be more popular with certain age groups and interests than others.

2. Set Clear Objectives: Define your social media goals by setting clear objectives. Do you want to promote your brand more, promote sales, or help customers?

3. Platform Research: It involves looking at the advantages and user bases of each platform. Different user bases and content types may be found on Facebook, Instagram, Twitter, LinkedIn, Pinterest, TikTok, and other platforms.

4. Analysis of Rivals: Examine the areas in which and the degree to which your rivals are engaged. Determine any areas where possibilities could be missing.

5. Material Suitability: Take into account the kind of material you'll be producing. While B2B firms succeed on LinkedIn, visual enterprises could do well on Instagram or Pinterest.

6. Resources and Capacity: Evaluate the abilities of your staff to properly handle numerous platforms. Always prioritize quality above quantity.

7. Content Calendar: Plan your content strategy and publishing schedule with the content calendar. Every platform has a recommended posting frequency for it.

8. Engagement and Interaction: Pick media outlets where you may interact with your audience directly. In social media, there is constant dialogue.

9. Options for Advertising: Examine each platform's advertising capabilities. Some people are more qualified than others for paid promotions.

10. Analytics and Metrics: Seek out platforms with strong analytics capabilities so you can monitor results and modify your plan as necessary.

11. Sector Relevance: Take into account forums or platforms that are specialized to your sector where your target audience may congregate.

12. Trend and Emerging Platforms: Emerging platforms and trends to watch out for include those that complement your brand. A competitive advantage might come from early adoption.

13. Trial and Error: Experimenting is OK. Start with a few platforms, evaluate their effectiveness, and gradually hone your plan.

14. Consistency: Maintain a consistent brand presence across all platforms by using a single voice and visual style.

15. Review and Adapt: Regularly evaluate your social media approach and make adjustments in response to changes in the social media environment or the behavior of your audience.

It's important to keep in mind that you should only be present on the platforms that are appropriate for your audience and your objectives. Making informed decisions guarantees that you put your time and money where they will have the most effect.

Producing Interesting Content

Forging strong relationships with your audience and grabbing their attention requires creating compelling content. Seven essential ideas to bear in mind are listed below:

1. **Know Your Audience:** To create content that meets your target audience's requirements, be aware of their interests, preferences, and pain areas.

2. Compelling Headlines: Create eye-catching headlines that arouse interest and entice people to read on.

3. Quality Visuals: Include high-quality pictures, videos, and graphics in your material to make it more appealing and help you get your point across.

4. Storytelling: Use compelling storylines to engross readers on an emotional level and leave them with a lasting impression of your message.

5. Clear Structure: Utilize headers, subheadings, and bullet points for a logical and clear structure that makes your text simple to read.

6. Call-To-Action (CAT): Encourage reader participation using calls to action (CTAs) that are obvious and direct readers to the next action, such as subscribing, sharing, or making a purchase.

7. **Consistency:** To establish familiarity and trust with your audience, maintain a consistent brand voice and style across all of your material.

You can develop content that not only captures your audience's attention but also keeps them interested and involved in your business by adhering to these rules.

Building a Social Media Community

An effective strategy for connecting with your audience, encouraging interaction, and fostering brand loyalty is to develop a flourishing social media community.

How to do it is as follows:

1. **Define Your Purpose:** Clarify the aims and purpose of your community by using

the phrase "define your purpose." Is it to provide customer service, to provide business ideas, or to build a following?

2. The Right Platforms: Choose social media sites where your target audience is engaged and where your material is in line with the strengths of each.

3. Create Valuable Content: Create informative, entertaining, or problem-solving material to share with your community. The key is consistency.

4. Engage Actively: Reply to comments, emails, and mentions as soon as possible. Talk to people in your neighborhood in a meaningful way.

5. Community Rules: Clearly define the rules of behavior in your community. Encourage pleasant encounters that are courteous.

6. User-Generated Content: Encourage community members to submit material by asking them to write reviews, testimonials, or user-generated pieces.

7. Exclusive Content or Rewards: Offer your community rewards in the form of exclusive material, webinars, or events. Make them feel cherished and valued.

8. Moderation: Keep an eye out for spam and objectionable material in your community. Apply your rules consistently.

9. Collaborate with Influencers: To increase your reputation and reach, team up with advocates or influencers in your neighborhood.

10. Surveys and Feedback: Seeking feedback is important for determining the needs and preferences of your community. Take surveys to learn more.

11. Recognize and Appreciate: acknowledge the efforts and accomplishments of other community members. Display user-generated material or endorsements.

12. Consistent Branding: Maintaining consistent Branding is essential for building a strong sense of identity within your neighborhood.

13. Data Analysis: To improve your strategy and content, analyze engagement metrics and community development.

14. Scaling with Moderators: As your community expands, think about employing moderators to assist with interaction management and keep a welcoming atmosphere.

15. Transparency: Be open and honest about your brand's goals and deeds in the neighborhood. Trust is important.

16. Evolve with Your Community:
Adjust your plan in light of the evolving
requirements and interests of your
community.

Although it takes time and effort to build a
social media community, the rewards are
worthwhile. A robust community can
support your business, provide insightful
criticism, and boost your success as a whole.

Use of User-Generated Content

User-generated content (UGC) is a useful
resource that may increase interaction with
and credibility for your business.

Here are some tips for using UGC:

**1. Encourage User-Generated Content
(UGC):** actively encourage people to create
and share material about your company, its
goods, or its services. As a way to encourage

involvement, use branded hashtags or questions.

2. Highlight Customer Stories: Share actual accounts and endorsements from happy clients. Showcase the beneficial effects your goods or services have had on their life.

3. Feature UGC on Your Platforms: Display UGC on your website, social network accounts, or marketing materials. Make sure you have the necessary authorizations and give creators credit.

4. Run UGC Campaigns: Host UGC competitions or campaigns with rewards like recognition or prizes. This could inspire people to produce and distribute content.

5. Collaborate With Influencers: Work together with influencers or brand evangelists who can create UGC and spread the word about your goods or services to their audience.

6. Share Authentic Stories: Share genuine UGC stories that are consistent with the goals and values of your company. Genuineness fosters trust.

7. Share the Behind-the-Scenes Contents: Share unpolished user-generated content. UGC doesn't have to be perfect. Share unvarnished or behind-the-scenes images that humanize your brand.

8. Join UGC Trends: Join trendy challenges or hashtags that are relevant to your brand to participate in user-generated content trends. Taking part in well-liked UGC trends might increase your reach.

9. Measure and Analyze: Track the effectiveness of UGC efforts, taking into account engagement, reach, and conversions. Refine your plan based on new information.

10. Legal Consideration: Be mindful of copyright and privacy concerns while using user-generated content (UGC). Always get the required approvals and offer due credit.

Utilizing user-generated content expands the audience for your business and fosters a feeling of belonging and authenticity for your goods and services. Encourage your audience to actively contribute to the creation of your brand's narrative.

Chapter 5

SEO (Search Engine Optimization)

Understanding Search Engine Optimization

Search engine optimization, or SEO, works like a secret code to make your website stand out in Google and other search engines.

Let's examine the fundamentals to discover its magic:

1. SEO: What is it?

SEO is a collection of methods to increase the visibility of your website in internet search results.

2. Why is it Significant?

Assume you own a wonderful store that is tucked away in a lonely lane. To help more people locate and visit your store (or website), SEO is like placing a sign on a major thoroughfare.

3. Keywords

These are the key keywords or terms that users enter into search engines. Consider these as hints. To match what people are looking for, you need to use the appropriate hints on your website.

4. Using On-Page SEO

This entails structuring and optimizing the content of your website. Use natural keyword placement in your headers, titles, and content. Make it simple to browse your website.

5. Using Off-Page SEO

It's similar to meeting friends online. Search engines understand that your website is trustworthy when they find links to it on other websites, particularly trustworthy ones.

6. High-Grade Content

Producing relevant, educational, and interesting information is essential. Websites that provide users value are highly favored by search engines.

7. Mobile-Friendly

Check that your website functions and looks fine on mobile devices. Google favors websites that are mobile-friendly.

8. Pages Per Second

Slow websites are disliked by everybody. A website that loads quickly makes both users and search engines pleased.

9. Meta Descriptions

These are succinct summaries of the information on your page. They may persuade users to click on your website since they show in search results.

10. Regional SEO

It's critical to optimize for local search if you own a local company. It makes you more discoverable to locals.

11. Analytics

Use tracking programs like Google Analytics to monitor the effectiveness of your website. It's comparable to finding out how many people visit your store every day.

12. Patience

SEO is a long-term strategy. Search engines take time to recognize your changes. Be persistent and patient.

13. Avoid Using Tricks

Some individuals use dubious methods to attempt to game the system. Search engines may punish your website as a result, which might backfire. Follow moral SEO guidelines.

14. Keep Updated

Like technology, SEO is always changing. Keep up with the most recent developments and trends in the SEO industry.

Essentially, SEO aims to make your website stand out in the internet space. It requires a blend of technical expertise, excellent content, and a little bit of patience.

You're well on your way to mastering the art of SEO by comprehending and putting these fundamentals into practice.

Keyword Analysis and Optimization

Effective SEO (Search Engine Optimization) is built on keyword research and optimization. Let's look at how these vital components combine to increase the visibility of your website in search engines:

Keyword Analysis

1. Knowing The Following Keywords
When searching for information online, users enter words or phrases known as keywords. They serve as a link between the services your website provides and the needs of consumers.

2. Relevance
The keywords you use for your article must be appropriate. "Running shoes for women" is more relevant if you offer shoes than "best ice cream flavors."

3. Volume Of The Search
To determine how often people search for certain terms, use tools like Google Keyword Planner or Ahrefs. Choose keywords that have a decent combination of relevant search volume.

4. Competition

Assess the level of competition for your preferred keywords. Consider both competitive and long-tail keywords since it may be difficult for new websites to rank for highly competitive keywords.

5. User Intention

Consider what consumers are looking for when they use a certain term. Are they seeking local services, goods, or information? Make your material specific to their objectives.

Optimizing Keywords

1. Optimization for On-Page Elements

Strategically include your target keywords in the title, headers, and body of your material. But keep it natural; don't fill it too much.

2. Meta Tags

Add relevant keywords to your meta title and meta description. These are the search results snippets that users view.

3. Content Caliber

Produce top-notch articles that aid people. Google rewards material that offers solutions to issues or offers insightful information.

4. Customer Experience

Ensure that your website is easy to use, responsive to mobile devices, and loads rapidly. User satisfaction might indirectly improve SEO.

5. Linking Internally

Include links to other pertinent pages on your website. In addition to assisting consumers, this distributes SEO "juice" across your website.

6. Backlinks

Gain links from trustworthy websites. Search engines see them as votes of confidence that indicate the authority of your website.

7. Regular Updates

Maintain current and new material. Google favors websites that provide up-to-date, relevant content.

8. Local SEO

If your company is based in a physical location, target local keywords like "best coffee shop in [your city]."

9. Monitoring And Analysis

Track your keyword ranks and traffic using programs like Google Analytics and Search Console. Adapt your plan in light of the results.

10. Avoid using Black Hat Techniques

Avoid unscrupulous strategies like purchasing backlinks or keyword stuffing. Search engine penalties may result from this.

Recall that SEO is a continuous effort. Review your keyword approach often, keep an eye on your ranks, and adjust as search engine algorithms change.

You'll increase your website's exposure and draw in more organic visitors with persistence and patience.

On-Page and Off-Page SEO

The dynamic duo of successful search engine optimization is on-page and off-page SEO.

A strong SEO strategy is built on the pillars of on-page and off-page optimization, which together increase your website's exposure and authority in search engine results.

Let's examine these fundamental elements:

Using On-Page SEO

1. Material Quality: On-page SEO begins with producing high-quality material that is relevant to and helpful to your audience. This includes descriptions of products, blog entries, articles, and more.

2. Keyword Optimization: Conduct keyword research and apply it to your advantage in the content, title, headers, and meta tags. Make sure the information is useful to readers and flows smoothly.

3. Meta Tags: Construct captivating meta titles and meta descriptions that faithfully summarize your content. These tags may affect click-through rates when they appear in search results.

4. Header Tags: (H1, H2, H3, etc.) may be used to organize your material. They facilitate the understanding of your content hierarchy by readers and search engines.

5. URL Structure: Construct neat, informative URLs that include keywords. Avoid using a lot of strange letters or lengthy numbers.

6. Internal Linking: Use internal links to lead visitors to other pertinent pages on your website. This improves site navigation and distributes SEO authority.

7. User Experience: Ensure that your website is responsive to mobile devices, loads swiftly, and provides a pleasant surfing experience. User-friendly websites are favored by search engines.

8. Image Optimization: Compress photos for quicker download and provide enlightening alt text. For SEO and accessibility, this is essential.

9. Material Updates: To keep your material current and correct, update it often. Google favors original material.

Using Off-Page SEO

1. Backlinks: Building backlinks from other websites to yours is the main goal of off-page SEO. These act as "votes" that represent the authority and trustworthiness of your website.

2. Quality Over Quantity: Pay attention to acquiring backlinks from reliable and relevant websites. A small number of high-quality backlinks are more influential than many low-quality ones.

3. Material Marketing: Produce material that is worth sharing and linking to since it inevitably generates backlinks. Linkable information includes things like infographics, in-depth tutorials, and research.

4. Social Signals: Social media participation and sharing have an indirect impact on off-page SEO. More backlinks may be obtained from popular material on social media networks.

5. Guest Posting: Contribute articles to reputable websites in your field. In your author profile, provide a link back to your website.

6. Online Reputation: Maintain a good internet reputation and reply to reviews and remarks, particularly for small firms. 6.

7. Competitor Analysis: Examine the backlink profiles of your rivals to find prospective prospects for link-building.

8. Disavow Spam Links: Conduct regular backlink audits and remove any spammy links that might hurt your SEO.

Keep in mind that both on-page and off-page SEO are crucial and work best together. Your website's optimized, high-quality content serves as the cornerstone for off-page SEO tactics like constructing reliable backlinks.

They all work together to raise your website's exposure and search engine rankings.

Measuring SEO Success

Tracking your website's performance in search engine rankings, organic visitor growth, and conversion rates are all important components of measuring SEO success.

It enables you to assess the success of your SEO efforts and make smart modifications to raise your brand's exposure and reach online.

Chapter 6

Collaborations and Partnerships

Locating strategic partners entails looking for companies or groups who share your objectives and can work together to achieve success. These collaborators should support your objective, aid in expanding your customer base, or improve your product offers.

Co-Marketing Techniques

Co-marketing, also known as "partnership marketing" or "collaborative marketing," is a potent tactic in which two or more companies collaborate to produce and market content or campaigns.

These alliances are advantageous to both sides and provide benefits to all parties.

Here is a thorough examination of co-marketing tactics:

1. Extending the Audience's Reach: Businesses may access one other's consumer bases via co-marketing. You may access a larger pool of prospective clients by collaborating with a business that caters to a similar target market but is not a direct rival.

2. Cost-Sharing: Marketing can be expensive, particularly for small firms. Through co-marketing, partners may split the cost of promotion, content production, and advertising. Both parties' costs may be greatly reduced as a result.

3. Diverse Expertise: Partnering with another company may help your marketing efforts by bringing in new ideas and knowledge. Combining these talents, for instance, might result in more successful campaigns if one partner is excellent at content production while the other is excellent at social media marketing.

4. Content Collaboration: Co-branding is often used to create ebooks, webinars, or films that are used in co-marketing. This material may be more thorough, attractive to your audience, and provide more value.

5. Enhanced Credibility: Working with a recognized partner may increase the credibility and dependability of your brand. Customers could consider your partnership with a reputable company to be a vote of confidence.

6. Cross-promotion: Cross-promotion is a key component of co-marketing, and it is mentioned in point number six. Sharing each other's blog articles, highlighting items in newsletters, or conducting webinars together are examples of this. These events make your company more widely known.

7. Utilizing Social Media: Co-marketing strategies often include coordinated social media advertising. Running joint competitions or exchanging content may increase engagement and interest on social media.

8. Determining Success: The performance of your co-marketing initiatives must be evaluated, just like any other marketing approach. To evaluate the success of your initiatives, keep track of indicators like website traffic, conversions, social media engagement, and customer acquisition.

9. Selecting the Ideal Partner: It's crucial to choose the best co-marketing partner. Find a company that aligns with your beliefs, target market, and marketing objectives. A collaboration that is well-aligned is more likely to produce fruitful outcomes.

10. Legal Arrangements: It is preferable to have written contracts in place that clearly define the obligations and expectations of each partner. Topics including income sharing, content ownership, and dispute resolution should be included in these agreements.

11. Ongoing Communication: Throughout the co-marketing collaboration, effective communication is essential. Share regular campaign updates, talk about changes, and take immediate action on any problems.

12. Establishing Long-Term Relationships: Co-marketing is not limited to one campaign. A network of useful connections in your sector may be created through establishing long-term relationships with partners, which can facilitate ongoing cooperation.

Legal and ethical considerations, including disclosures in sponsored material, are addressed in number thirteen. - Ensure compliance with all relevant laws and regulations. Keep up moral marketing standards to safeguard the image of your company.

Co-marketing is a dynamic technique that, when done well, may provide enormous rewards. It's about using your partners' talents to develop more effective marketing campaigns and accomplish shared objectives.

Exploring co-marketing options may be a wise step to increase your brand's exposure and reach, whether you're a tiny startup or an established company.

Measurement of Partnership Impact

To evaluate partnerships' efficacy and make wise choices, it is essential to measure their impact.

Here's how to gauge the effect of your collaborations:

1. KPI Tracking: Identify and monitor certain Key Performance Indicators (KPIs) that are in line with partnership objectives, such as website traffic, conversion rates, and income made.

2. Conversion Analysis: Evaluate conversion rates and customer acquisition costs (CAC) for traffic coming from the partnership and compare them to those coming from other marketing channels.

3. Customer Feedback: Collect information via surveys or feedback forms to see how consumers learned about your company and if the collaboration affected their choice.

4. Social and Web Analytics: Keep track of social media activity and web analytics to determine the effect of partnered promotions, content, and referral traffic.

5. ROI Evaluation: Determine the return on investment (ROI) by weighing the advantages of the relationship (revenue, leads, brand exposure) against the disadvantages.

It is necessary to take a complete approach when evaluating the effects of partnerships, including quantitative and qualitative data.

You may leverage the advantages and accomplish your company objectives by routinely evaluating and changing your collaboration tactics.

Ensuring Mutually Beneficial Relationships

Long-term success in partnerships requires ensuring connections that are advantageous to both parties. Both sides must cooperate well to accomplish this, with each party benefiting from the partnership.

1. Specify Your Expectations and Goals: Establish specific objectives and expectations for the cooperation right away. Make sure that everyone is aware of their obligations and goals.

2. Open Communication: Encourage free and honest conversation. Update each other often on developments, difficulties, and possibilities. To have a good working connection, resolve any difficulties right away.

3. Fair Contributions: Ensure that both parties provide a fair share of their resources to the partnership. A balanced contribution promotes a feeling of justice, whether it be in terms of resources, knowledge, or marketing initiatives.

4. Shared Advantages: Indicate the advantages of the collaboration to each side. It can be easier access to a new audience, more money, or more brand reputation. Make sure that all parties see concrete benefits.

5. Adaptability and Flexibility: Partnerships may develop over time, and conditions can alter. To maintain a relationship that benefits both parties, be adaptable and open to change in response to new possibilities or problems.

6. Regular Evaluation: Regularly evaluate the partnership's progress toward its original objectives. Adjust the terms or methods as necessary if the rewards are not distributed fairly.

7. Mutual Courtesy: Develop a connection built on trust and respect for one another. Recognize and value each other's efforts and accomplishments.

8. Conflict Resolution: Establish a procedure for settling disputes peacefully. An amicably resolved conflict might make the relationship stronger.

9. Long-Term Vision: Take into account the partnership's long-term potential. Long-term gains and partnerships may result from developing strong ties.

Businesses may create and sustain relationships that are not only beneficial but also based on trust, respect, and shared success by giving priority to these concepts.

Chapter 7

Conclusion

Important Strategies

1. Understanding Your Audience: To successfully focus your marketing efforts, be aware of the preferences, requirements, and demographics of your target audience.

2. Content Creation: Produce compelling material of the highest caliber for your target viewers. Think about email newsletters, social media updates, and blog postings.

3. Making Use of User-Generated Content: Encourage readers to comment and provide reviews. To establish credibility and trust, use their endorsements.

4. Email Marketing: To keep readers interested, create and manage an email list.

Send frequent updates, privileged content, and marketing materials.

5. Social Media Engagement: Engage in social media to communicate with readers, distribute material, and carry out specialized advertising efforts.

6. Website Optimization: Make sure your author's website is user-friendly, has interesting material, and is SEO-optimized.

7. Analytics and Monitoring: Utilize analytics and data technologies to monitor the success of your marketing initiatives and make fact-based choices.

8. Innovation and Adaptation: Keep up with market developments, modify your plans, and research fresh marketing ideas.

Keep in mind that effective marketing is a constant process that demands commitment and consistent work. To get the greatest results, adapt these tactics and you will be glad you do.

9 798886 244584